ROCK

By S.L. Hamilton

VISIT US AT
ABDOPUBLISHING.COM

Published by ABDO Publishing Company, 8000 West 78th Street, Suite 310,
Edina, MN 55439. Copyright ©2011 by Abdo Consulting Group, Inc. International
copyrights reserved in all countries. No part of this book may be reproduced
in any form without written permission from the publisher. A&D Xtreme™ is a
trademark and logo of ABDO Publishing Company.

Printed in the United States of America, North Mankato, Minnesota.
112010
012011

 PRINTED ON RECYCLED PAPER

Editor: John Hamilton
Graphic Design: Sue Hamilton
Cover Design: John Hamilton
Cover Photo: Getty
Interior Photos: Alamy-pgs 12 & 24; AP-pgs 15, 17, 18, 19, 23, 28 & 29;
Corbis-pgs 9, 11, 13, 16, 17 & 22; Getty Images-pgs 1, 4, 5, 6, 7, 8,
10, 11, 14, 15, 16, 17, 19, 20, 21, 26 & 27; Paramount Pictures-pg 12;
ThinkStock-pgs 2, 3, 22, 23, 24, 25, 30 & 31.

Library of Congress Cataloging-in-Publication Data

Hamilton, Sue L., 1959-
  Rock / S.L. Hamilton.
     p. cm. -- (Xtreme dance)
  ISBN 978-1-61714-733-3
  1. Rock and roll dancing--Juvenile literature. I. Title.
  GV1796.R6H36 2011
  793.3--dc22
                              2010037648

CONTENTS

XTREME

For more than 60 years, the rhythmic drumbeats and screaming guitars of rock 'n' roll music have brought dancers to their feet.

ROCKIN'

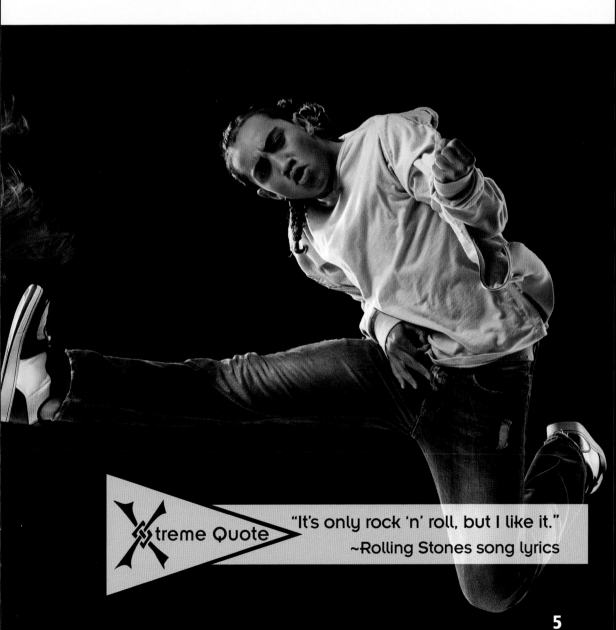

Xtreme Quote

"It's only rock 'n' roll, but I like it."
~Rolling Stones song lyrics

ROCK

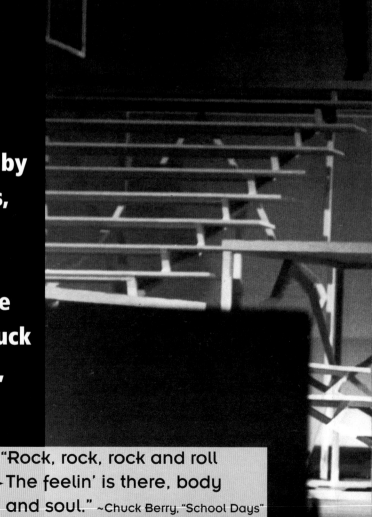

Rock and roll is a blend of blues, jazz, country, and gospel styles of music. With a big backbeat created by drums and guitars, early rock music rose in popularity in the 1950s. Dance crazes, such as Chuck Berry's Duck Walk, soon followed.

HISTORY

Chuck Berry's Duck Walk

"I did the Duck Walk the first time to hide the wrinkles in my suit. It got an ovation, so I did it again and again."

DANCE

1950s

Elvis
Presley

In the 1950s, Elvis Presley's rock music and swivel-hip dance style was popular. Teens also learned to "dance" with their hands. The Hand Jive, a series of hand moves and claps, was performed to rock and roll music.

STYLES

Xtreme Fact

In London, England, dance floors were too crowded to move, so teens Hand Jived to the music.

1960s

The Twist was a dance style created by singer Chubby Checker in the early 1960s. It was one of the first dance styles to have couples dancing apart from each other. This became the standard for future rock dances. Other 1960s dances such as the Jerk, the Pony, the Watusi, and the Mashed Potato were based on the Twist.

"The Twist is dancing apart to the beat. You're doing something together but you're not touching."

Chubby Checker's Twist

The Watusi

The Mashed Potato

1970s

The Hustle

John Travolta

Disco music hit the dance scene in the 1970s. Rockers moved to disco's electronic beat with such dances as the Bump and the Hustle. Dancers bumped hips in the Bump. John Travolta made the Hustle famous in the movie *Saturday Night Fever*. In the same decade, rock musicians and fans started the Headbanging dance style.

The Bump

Headbanging may have begun with the rock group Led Zeppelin.

Xtreme Fact

Headbanging causes head and neck pain. Doctors advise rockers to limit head motion.

1980s

In the 1980s, Michael Jackson popularized many of the pop-rock era's dances. Some of Jackson's moves included the Toe Stand, Circle Spin, and Moonwalk. Entertainer MC Hammer's Hammer Dance and Tina Turner's powerful high-heeled rock moves were famous.

Michael Jackson's Toe Stand.

Xtreme Fact Michael Jackson, MC Hammer, and Tina Turner were listed on the Top 25 Dancers of All Time by BET Network.

The Hammer Dance is also called the Typewriter Dance.

MC Hammer

Tina Turner

1990s

Madonna's Vogue

Voguing became a popular dance style with Madonna's hit song "Vogue" in 1990. The dance featured hand movements and model-like poses. Music videos of the 1990s highlighted the dance moves of such music artists as Prince, Janet Jackson, and Will Smith. In 1996 Los Del Río's song "Macarena" became a #1 hit dance single.

Macarena

Prince

Janet Jackson

Will Smith

17

2000s

Jennifer Lopez

Ricky Martin

Jennifer Lopez and Ricky Martin put Latin dance moves into their shows during the beginning of the 21st century. Dancers used hip-hop moves made popular by performers such as Sean "Diddy" Combs and Nelly. Moshing, or packed group dancing, grew in popularity at live concerts. Rockers often crowd surfed over mosh pits.

Diddy

Nelly

Crowd surfing over a mosh pit.

2010s and On

Beyoncé

Strong performers such as Lady Gaga and Beyoncé mix many dance styles. Their dances often include bold lighting and wild costumes. Today's dancers use athletic moves and fist-pumping dramatics to groove to modern rock rhythms.

Lady Gaga

ROCKIN'

Fashion changed to allow people to dance to the music of the era.

1950s

1960s

FASHION

1980s

2000s

Hair & Hats

Hairstyles and hat fashions have changed along with rock and roll. From long to short hair, from crewcut to mohawk, rock dancers use their hair as part of the rhythmic identity of rock and roll.

LEARN

Dance schools teach moves to newcomers. Many people watch and copy the moves found on music videos and at dance clubs. Internet instructions for dances are often found on YouTube, Dance Advantage, and Dancejam.

TO ROCK

DANCE

Many cities and Web sites hold dance contests, such as Body Rock or YouTube Dance Studio.

CONTESTS

THE

Disco
A popular dance music with a strong bass beat. Disco was commonly heard and danced to in the 1970s.

Era
A period of time, usually measured in months or years.

Gospel
A religious style of music that features strong rhythms and uplifting lyrics. Gospel's beginnings are credited to the singing and dancing styles of African-Americans in the southern United States.

Led Zeppelin
A British hard rock band formed in 1968. Members included Jimmy Page (guitar), Robert Plant (vocals), John Paul Jones (guitar/keyboards), and John Bonham (drums). Fans and members of the group are credited with originating headbanging. The group disbanded in 1980 after the death of John Bonham. The band was inducted into the Rock and Roll Hall of Fame in 1995.

GLOSSARY

Macarena
A dance and song by the Spanish group Los del Río.
The song became a major hit in the mid-1990s, and
continues to be played at dances.

Mosh Pit
An area near the front of a live band performance
where audience members gather closely to dance
to the music.

Pop-Rock
A lighter, catchy style of rock music. Usually guitar-
based, pop-rock is often more upbeat.

Rolling Stones
A British rock group that first became popular in the
1960s, and continues to perform today. The band
was inducted into the Rock and Roll Hall of Fame
in 1989. Today, members of the group include Mick
Jagger (vocals), Keith Richards (guitar), Ronnie
Wood (guitar/bass), and Charlie Watts (drums).

INDEX

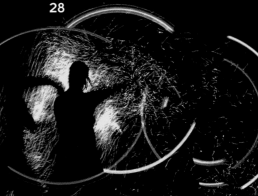